CRASH COURSE

CRASH COURSE

ESTEBAN RODRIGUEZ

SADDLE ROAD PRESS

Crash Course © 2019 Esteban Rodriguez

Saddle Road Press
Hilo, Hawai'i
saddleroadpress.com

All rights reserved. No part of this book may be reproduced or transmitted in any form or by any means without written permission of the author.

Book design by Don Mitchell
Cover photograph by María Elena Pérez
Author photograph by Sarah Eads

ISBN 978-1-7329521-3-3

To my mother, sister, and father

Contents

Y2K	9
Ink	11
Ode to Tupperware	12
MacGyver	13
Cankles	14
Boots	15
Shadow	17
Piel	18
CPR	19
Photograph, 1996	20
Clan	21
Ode to my Father's Wife Beater	22
Golden Years	23
Hide	24
Goldfish	25
Grito	26
Parable	27
Inglés	28
Bio	29
Auto-shop	30
Onan	31

K.O.	32
Kicks	35
AI	41
Hair	42
Hands	43
Mercy	44
Refuge	45
Fingernail	46
Herpes	47
Temptation	48
Segue	49
Leftovers	50
Coca-Cola	52
Boils	53
Psychic	54
VHS	55
Seeds	56
Baywatch	57
Stroke	58
Pit Stop	59
Date Night	60
La chupacabra	61
Backtalk	62
Ode to Glitter	63
Titanic	64
Acknowledgments	65
About the Author	67

Y2K

Because every computer was going to die,
and software would become a relic
overnight, my father packed a survival kit,
bought extra water, canned food,
cartridges for a shotgun he feared
he'd have to use, warning of *asesinos*,
ladrones, of a desperation that would lead us
to do things we thought we'd never do.
And so we waited, and instead of going outside,
starting a barbecue, watching the fireworks
light up the neighborhood, we huddled
in the living room, pretended it was a basement,
pretended what we were seeing on TV
wasn't real, that the crowd in Times Square—
never mind in Australia or New Zealand—
was, according to my father, prerecorded
propaganda, paid for by the government
to hide the truth, which, as the night carried on,
I was unsure about, confused as to what
was really true. And maybe I made all this up,
maybe there was no kit, no paranoia,
that that evening my father was just tired,
and so was my mother, and because they'd been
on their feet all day, they wanted, even
as the century was about to end, to sit,
rest, to believe that as they watched
the celebrations, they were still a part of them,
that they were there to witness the world
stay exactly the same.

INK

Tupac preaches, and near his voice
I sit, watching one cousin tattoo
the other, watching smoke fill the room,
until all I see is a needle, a name,
a script that curls and spreads across
Lalo's chest, like branches, tentacles,
like roots replacing the root-shaped flare
of his veins. But when the blood settles,
and the walls have grayed, I think
of the ink as armor, a badge, as a medal
he won for loving his girl, and for turning,
days before, the name of his ex into a flag,
thick, botched, snake- and eagle-less,
more Italian than Mexican, but large enough
to tell us that the past could be erased,
or at least covered, masked with thick lines,
bold colors, or with whatever image
he could buy for his flesh, knowing
there'd be no regrets.

Ode to Tupperware

No party. No spread. No living room
filled with coworkers, neighbors, friends.
No Tupperware really, just cabinets stacked
with plastic bowls, containers, lids,
with generic brands your mother buys
on discount, packs and seals leftovers in.
And when you open the fridge, adjust
to the light erasing midnight off your skin,
you rummage the shelves, find old chicken,
potatoes, eggs, find that spaghetti your mother
makes when she wants to feel European,
or less like a clichéd Mexican woman
who, after cleaning a house that's already clean,
enters the kitchen, cooks rice and beans,
labors over a dinner your father comes home to,
critiques with a head shake that says,
Not this again, or if his day was bad,
by pouring salt before he takes a bite,
so as to say to your mother, *Fuck you*,
so as to say to you, *Eat this at your own risk*,
which you do, and which you return to
at night, picking at something that tastes
like meat, until you find you've scraped
the whole container clean.

MacGyver

Then the handle broke,
and when the window sunk,
and we could no longer pull
the rest of it up, my father cut
a trash bag, taped it on the door,
made the car look as though
it had an eye patch, or as though—
when the bag billowed, fluttered
like a sail—it was a small boat,
or was whatever metaphor I made
that my father didn't understand,
just as he didn't know who MacGyver
was, and why, every time he taped
the bumper back on, glued the fallen
side view mirror, or kicked the grille
so the car would start, I called him
a name so *gringo*, *americano*,
bestowed him with a compliment
he shrugged off, never once asking
what it meant, and thinking perhaps
that when I stood behind him,
watched him wave the smoke
from the hood, nicknames did little
to get things fixed.

Cankles

Our mothers had them.
And when our sisters grew
into our mothers' bodies,
dressed like they had a house,
husband, children to take care of,
we thought they plagued
only women in our family,
until one day we looked
more closely, saw them
on our uncles, saw how
they mixed with diabetes:
bruised, swollen, scaly,
like the skin of some alien species,
or of a human after an alien
takes over its body, and unable
to hold such a being, begins
to break, fill the cuts and cracks
with liquid we weren't sure
how to name, just as we
didn't know what to call
the feeling of standing
next to a hospital bed, staring
at one of our uncles, wondering
why half his leg was gone,
and why our mothers whispered
amongst themselves
that his chances were slim,
that when he woke up earlier,
asked if they could scratch
his ankle, they couldn't answer,
couldn't bear to place their hands
on that part of him that still itched.

Boots

Sunday. And here you are again:
la pulga, that labyrinth of stands
your grandparents led you
through as a boy, searching,
for hours, for the cheapest sacks
of garlic, for tomatoes, oranges,
for handheld radios and car parts
that your grandfather, according
to your grandmother's crossed
arms and silence, had no use for,
which is why your father, minutes in,
loses your mother, knowing that even
if he swore not to open his wallet,
she'll object to everything he looks at.
You follow, watch him peruse booths
hawking belt buckles, pocket knives,
watches, chains with gold crosses,
rings with stones you once believed
told the future. You look too, mistake
for a second the leather for genuine,
the blades for sturdy, the gilded Christs
for humble, holy, and as you start
to think, as you've thought before,
that maybe the food you smell
is the only thing authentic, your father
turns the corner, strolls toward a booth
whose shelves are stacked with boots
made of ostrich, crocodile, snakeskin,
seeing in each pair a young version
of himself, a man who, dressed
in a cowboy hat and Wranglers,
stands in the corner of some cantina,

watching the couples dance, and waiting
till a song he knows comes on,
till his body begins to move, loose
and with nothing to hold it back.

Shadow

And when they got him to stay,
calmed his barking, excitement,
they took turns scratching his belly,
legs, until my oldest cousin—adamant
that with animals no part of this
was technically gay—moved his hand
to Shadow's penis, stroking it slowly,
calmly, with purpose we ourselves
were still learning, with the intent
of reaching the same silent ending,
because Shadow, like us, would feel better
once it was done, or so my cousins
claimed, and so on nights when I slept
over, and we lay exhausted in bed,
I'd replay the end of this scene,
wonder if bodies this close to each other
should feel what shouldn't be named.

Piel

Begin with adjectives: brown, bronze,
dark as old leather left out in the sun.
And as you pick a scene and dust
the edges off, focus on the bridge
crossing back, on the beggars you still hear
when you and your mother reach the end,
open a door and feel the rush of cool
office air, and wait, as you've waited before,
for the line to dwindle, for the officer
to call you up, ask for your papers,
and pause when he takes in your mother's
skin, then looks at yours, unconvinced
your light complexion makes you
her son. Remember your silence,
remember the questions that sound,
from what little Spanish you understand,
like they're meant for your mother
to slip, to stutter the wrong birthday,
birthplace, the full name that still gets stuck
on your lips. And when the officer
turns to you, asks in a heavy accent
if this woman is really your mom,
nod and say yes, then grab your mother's
hand, sure that your touch will be enough
to let you both pass.

CPR

Manikin splayed, and we kneel
beside it. And because its torso
is bare, and its chest—ordinary, pale—
is still that of a man, your friends laugh,
wait till the teacher turns around,
and together, with all their strength,
grab the back of your head, force it down,
expecting you to give in, to kiss
those plastic lips, reveal to everyone
that the rumors they spread were true:
you liked men, couldn't resist the imitation
of a man in front of you. And though
you can only guess what they think,
you believe they know that when you pull
away, part of you wants to tell of those
spin-the-bottle nights, of the fate
that picked you, then them, of the awkward
laugh meant to disguise every time
horseplay went too far, and you found
your mouths near, speechless and breathing
way too fast, hard.

Photograph, 1996

One goat. Two goats.
Three goats dead in the field.
And when you find the fourth one,
cold and anointed with flies,
your father makes you pose with it,
directs you, with the camera
in his hand, to straddle its back,
grab its horns, like a trophy,
like a prize. You do as you're told,
and as your father kneels, adjusts
the lens, you ponder what images
live only in his head: the blurry,
midnight bouts with the wall,
days filled with rebar, plywood,
stubborn cement. And you're certain
that if you search back far enough,
unveil the silent layers of his mind,
you'll find him on a hot, summer night,
standing at his country's edge, ready,
even if he barely knows how to swim,
to dive into the river again, give
the last leg of his trek another try,
and if the current isn't greedy
with him, to feel, when he reaches
the other side, like someone new,
which is why on days like these,
when a carcass appears on the field,
he can be, if just for an afternoon,
more photographer than father,
more than willing to let you
lift a dead goat's head, certain
he'll capture more than just death.

Clan

At night she sang: lullaby, prayer,
the same song she'd start, but never finish,
thinking that when my eyes became
heavy, and my cheek kissed the pillow,
there was no longer a need for lyrics,
that she had nothing more for me
than a kiss for my forehead. And when
she'd lean over, brush aside my hair,
I'd catch a glimpse of her chin, neck,
then let my eyes wander to her breasts,
not knowing what that part of her body
meant, but aware that it was different,
that although it was swollen, shaped
and shaded with the force of my father's
hands, it was so unembarrassed, worn
with a knowledge that this was the only flesh
she had, and there was no need to feel shame
for someone else's choices, much less
for the wrinkles, darkness, for the stretch marks
light enough to make it seem like the markings
of an ancient tribe, one she was no longer
a part of, but whose traditions she still practiced,
and which she'd carry out if it meant
protecting her son, no matter how ugly
the setting, no matter how calm.

Ode to my Father's Wife Beater

Sundays they hung, wrinkled, wet,
faithful to the wind's fingertips,
or to mine when, bored and still dressed
in a button-down and slacks, I'd imagine
them as albino bats, or as skinned raccoons,
rats, or as whatever strange, undersized
creature that wasn't the wife beater
my father wore at the house, walking in it
like it was chain mail, and like he had just
returned from war, slayed the regime
of a 12-hour shift—that oppressiveness
of laying rebar, cement, of bearing the sun—
his ancient enemy—on the singed armor
of his skin. And because he won,
and walked away with enough of himself
left, he came home eager for rewards:
dinner, TV, beer, space and family silence,
and the right to not care about the sweat
stained on his chest, or the way he smelled,
gave off a scent that I—those Sunday
afternoons—inhaled, thinking that if I tiptoed
higher, pressed my nose against the fabric,
I'd feel, for a moment, his body near.

Golden Years

Because nursing homes were for *gringos*,
my grandfather spent his last years
on the couch, idle, silent, drooling
as he watched *novelas*, old episodes
of *Cops*, and—as hour after hour passed—
never once blinking, even when I snuck up,
flashed my silliest faces in front of his eyes.
Like a monk, or the Queen's Guard,
he remained stoic, lost in his thoughts,
and indifferent when my father, out of habit,
asked if he was hungry, if he wanted to eat
with us. And though he said nothing,
signaled neither yes or no when he grunted,
coughed, my father nodded to me for help,
and together, with our arms on his torso,
back, we lifted the limp mass he'd become,
carried him to the table, as though we were dragging
a soldier, a brother we tried to comfort,
knowing that no matter how much we whispered
Hang on, hang on, whatever was left of him
would never make it home.

Hide

November. And because your father's
out of work again, you hide clothes
in whatever store you find yourself in,
stuff shirts, shorts, and underwear toward
the back of racks, shelves, not because
you want them, but because your mother does,
and you know—now that you're older,
now that you realize layaway is a luxury—
that you owe her for every action figure
you once begged for, for the times you cried,
screamed, cried, screamed, until she,
exhausted with the sound of her *No's*,
agreed, threw them in the cart, demanding
in return that you try on clothes she'd already
picked out, and that you didn't pout when they fit,
or didn't smile when they were too tight, loose,
and when she, in order to save face and time,
had to leave them in the dressing room,
abandoned in the same way she abandons
a blouse she presses to her chest, and,
after running the week's budget through
her head, puts back on the rack, knowing
that we shouldn't be here, but that it doesn't
hurt to look, that we can love things
without owning them, that we can pray
we'll someday return.

Goldfish

You find it bobbing,
mouth open, eyes wide,
vacant. And before you think
of your grandfather, the night
the machines went silent,
the moment he gasped, stopped
breathing, you remember
the chicks, the box they laid in,
sprawled, one against the other,
as if they were sleeping,
as if the trails of shit beside them—
brown and bloodied—didn't mean
anything, just as you told yourself
the worms in your puppy's feces
were nothing really, that all dogs
were born with them, and that once
they were out, left to writhe
like newborns on the ground,
Max would be normal again,
no yelping, limping, no swaying
like he was drunk, not making you
feel the way you feel now, numb
and unsure if goldfish should be
buried or flushed.

Grito

For every speech, toast.
For every wedding where fathers
and grandfathers gathered, drank
and watched younger men blur
on the dance floor. For the wedding
itself. For the husband, wife.
For the secret bets waged how soon
they'd get divorced. Hell,
for every mother-in-law too,
and for the way you, anytime birthdays
or backyard barbecues occur,
end up by your uncles and cousins,
aware of how much younger you are,
but of how you're willing to bear
the jokes, the head shakes and smirks
if it means you're allowed to be here,
or that they'll attempt to teach you
how to belt one out, explain,
in a Spanish too tipsy to really know,
that you must crank your neck,
relax your mouth, that it must not come
from the throat, but the gut, the soul,
from whatever lives between your heart
and lips, and that once released, sent
to the tip of your tongue, will fill
the smoky air, wake, for all you care,
the whole damn neighborhood up.

Parable

Summer. Barbecue. A backyard
with a pool. And near it you find
your father, in shades, shorts,
with a beer in hand because today
is his day off, and on days off
he acts younger, willing to banter
with his brothers, to sacrifice sternness
for laughter, to offer you, when you
approach, a compliment in Spanish,
and then, in an English his tongue,
even after decades of building plazas
in this country, hasn't quite mastered,
teases you, says you need more sun,
says that your skin—night and day
when compared to his—looks pale,
transparent, like that of some exotic fish,
which leads him, you believe, to ask
if you know how to swim. And though
you shake your head, he hammers the air
with the question again, again, knowing
that you can probably float, and that,
in order to save face, to prove to your uncles
he wasn't raising a son who was scared,
he shoves your chest, laughs when you fall in,
shouts something you can't make out,
but which you think, as you slap the water,
let chlorine baptize your throat, is *Sorry*,
an apology that there is no lesson
for you to learn, that when you manage
to grab the ledge, pull yourself up,
you'll have missed your chance
to claim you've been reborn.

Inglés

A car cuts us off, and my mother yells,
Fuck you, beach! Then rants in Spanish.
She honks again, again, says to me,
Here, everyone bad drivers. And I nod,
let out a nervous laugh, and consider
not just how hard she slams the pedal,
or that her eyes reach just above the wheel,
but the confidence she's gained with English,
her willingness to curse, yell what
she still can't pronounce, unlike me
trying to learn her language, which,
at school, I fumble, forgetting that *es*
is not *está*, that nouns are gendered,
or that when I script lines for my side
of a paired conversation, I should speak
in my best accent, should guide every word
carefully across the borders of my mouth.

Bio

Slowly, you take one out,
splay it on your tray, wait for lab
to start, watch your classmates
toss their frogs around—
like it's all a game, like they know
something funny about death
that you haven't figured out yet—
something your father understood
the weekends he took you to hunt
and which he tried to instill back
at home, taking a bird from the ice
chest, clipping its wings, ripping
its head, then, without so much
as a nod, lobbing the feathered mass
into your lap, unable not to laugh when,
after plucking the kill clean, you stuck
your thumb up the ass, pulled
what remained apart, so that all
you were left with was a warm,
BB-riddled chunk of meat, a secret
you had no choice but to keep.

Auto-shop

Days he gave the engine a rest,
your cousin polished the rims,
made sure dust and dirt didn't blur
his reflection. And how clearly
you saw yours when, after school
one afternoon, he rode through
the pick-up lane, windows down,
Tupac on, hydraulics in full effect.
And as he bounced closer,
bumpers scraping the pavement,
you didn't feel, as you later would,
shame or embarrassment, but pride
that you were leaving, at least once
this year, in style, noticed
by teachers, potential girlfriends,
friends, all seen in those shiny rims,
and all clueless about the work
your cousin put in, how—
twenty-something years old,
working part time and still living
at home—he learned what he knew
about cars all by himself, and poured
enough time into his to revel in
the whispers, stares, in the belief
that as he turned the music up,
opened the door, he wasn't just doing
your mom a favor, but was making
a statement, peeling out with a sense
of vindication.

Onan

Midway through, religion kicks in,
and you picture your place in hell,
the pit where masturbators
are thrown, screaming, crying,
begging for forgiveness, writhing
on the ground without their limbs.
And yet, as you see yourself amongst
them, pleading to a god who no longer
listens, you don't stop, try not think
about your judgment, how fire
will feel against your flesh,
or that your sin, as you've heard
televangelists claim, is the catalyst
for larger events: poverty, hurricanes,
ongoing wars and every end-of-the-world
disease. And with every stroke,
there are new victims, calamities:
your grandfather's memory,
your aunt's car accident, and, as always,
your mother's sudden blindness,
the way she doesn't see you
when she walks in, turns away
from the power shrinking quickly
in your hand.

K.O.

It begins with a pillow—
light hit, light toss, the light
smothering of your temples,
mouth. Then, when old enough,
it's boxing gloves, the impromptu
ring of a backyard. And though
you punch in jest, move your feet
and feign the motions, your father
doesn't, jabbing barehanded,
throwing hooks so your body
hardens, so it learns to endure
whatever flesh means to harm it:
right fist, left fist, right fist, left,
or the back of his hands you bear
on nights he eggs you on, shoving,
swinging, swaying back and forth
and back, slurring, in between each sip,
a speech you can't understand,
but which you take to mean,
even when he won't stop, that this—
all of it—is not the man
you should become.

KICKS

After Converse, you jump ship,
devote yourself to Dr. Martens.
And though your first pair's
a hand-me-down, worn and a size
too big, you take a Sharpie, fill in
the creases, cracks, avoid the sunlight
when you're out, so no one sees
the vitiligo shades of black,
doesn't think, like you do,
that your boots resemble leopard fur,
only not as fierce, and not as bold
as the pairs other boys wear, looking,
with their pants tight, torn
and rolled, as if they were ready
to march, were willing to burn
every place they entered down.

~

You ask for Js, explain
the need for grip, describe
the way you slide across
the court, stumble, trip,
and still your father gifts
you cleats, hopes, without
saying what he feels,
that you'll give his sport
a second chance. And so
you do, and in the yard,
unsure how to aim your feet,
you kick the ball, watch
your father kick it back,
listen—as you try to dribble,

strike it smoothly across
the grass—to how sudden
he becomes a coach,
shouting, pointing, correcting
your angle of attack,
and insisting, through
a language of head shakes
and moans, that you try again,
that you never think some things
are worth more in their box.

~

For kicks, you try one on, lift
your pants, flash your foot in the mirror.
Then, because your father's asleep,
and your mother's in the kitchen,
burdened, as always, with doing
motherly things, you take off your socks,
put both heels on, and strut, half-jokingly,
like the models you've seen on TV,
or like the ones in the magazines
your mother never reads, but which,
when she's not around, you flip through,
imagine each body in motion,
imagine yourself shaped
with such poise, curves, and with
confidence you reinterpret, welcome
no matter how much it hurts.

~

Not the Js you wanted,
but the second best.
Or the third. Hell, you'll take
the fourth if it means
you're not the boy picked last,
not the one the captains,

decked in Nikes or Airs,
tilt their heads at, unsure
where they know you from,
whose brother you belong to,
whose cousin can vouch
on your behalf. No. Not the Js
you wish you had, but these,
AND1s, bulky, black, so heavy
you think you're wearing clogs,
but with less history, finesse,
with a ruggedness that says
you'll dive, call out your man,
box whoever's near out,
and, because you're more heart
than skill, reach for every bad
shot, even if your body
never leaves the ground.

~

Like fate, destiny, like a noun
that gives you every reason
to be here, you rummage
your parents' closet, ignore
the heels you once wore, ignore
the sandals, stench, bear the mess
you make until you find your father's
work boots, worn, unused for years,
and all yours if you want them,
if you decide, as graduation nears,
that you don't want a life of libraries,
classes, of walking from one building
to the next, in awe of their architecture,
but never thinking of who built them,
of the men who, like your father,
woke up early every morning,

ready to trek a maze of wood,
rebar, pipes and wet cement,
and ready not only for the heat,
but for any change in weather,
for something as simple as rain
to dock a day from their checks.

~

Not the latest, nor the ones
talked about, envied,
but a pair nonetheless,
black on white, fitted, fresh,
as comfy as you expect
Js to be. And not just
for practice, or for the few
minutes you come off the bench,
but for school, Saturday nights
at home, dressed and convinced
your phone will ring. Yes,
for any chance to show off
your kicks, to claim your seat
at the table. And though
you don't know exactly
what this phrase means,
you know enough to wear
your Js any time, place:
sidewalk, gravel, the mornings
the ground outside your house
is blessed with rain, and the few,
long minutes it takes to reach
the bus, to keep what you've poured
your pride into clean.

AI

Then came the Age of Doubt,
the belief you held for weeks
that your mother wasn't human,
that she was made of more than flesh
and bone, that when the iron slipped—
the tip of it kissing her palms or wrists—
she was programmed to suppress
her jerks, squeals, moans, to never
acknowledge the hole being seared
through her skin. No, she gave no mistake
the reaction it deserved, too focused
on your father's pants and shirts,
on erasing creases, wrinkles,
on bringing order to the crumpled chaos
of your polos, shorts. And because
she never noticed you were near,
you walked to the board when she
was done, plugged the iron back in,
and placed your hand on the plate,
knowing each time that it would burn,
that you'd run to your mother afterwards,
show her how fragile your body was,
and watch her rub the wound with clumps
of Vaseline, wondering, as she lathered
more in, if there were more like her,
if the heart she had could be found
in other machines.

Hair

As my father's hair fell out,
left a bald spot I thought brought
luck if whispered to or rubbed,
my mother's thinned in front,
revealed the frailty of her widow's
peak, that her scalp, except for redness,
dandruff, looked just as tragic
as any other man's. And still,
even when *canas* took root,
and her body began to shrivel,
she remained committed to her hair,
combed it in the morning down the middle,
put it in a ponytail in the afternoon,
or, when she felt lonely and unloved,
she'd try her hand at bangs till they looked
like the bristles of a worn broom.
And I would say, any time
my friends gazed too long, that she
was in recovery, that the chemo
made her frail, ate up all her hair,
and that only now, after being in
and out of hospitals for years,
was she looking like herself again,
ready to end a battle we thought
she'd never win.

Hands

And when he grabbed my arm,
pushed me against the wall, I thought
of him at work, of the way his spine
would bend, contort, invent new
geometries, twist in angles I had never
felt. I thought of his grip, of the decades
of calluses, of how his palms resembled
rust, or tree bark, or the caliche splayed
into a semblance of a road outside
our house. And though I knew
he had to use gloves, I pictured my father
barehanded, moving bricks, rebar,
lifting 2x4s and slabs of wood,
conditioned to the repetition, weight,
and to the pain that came when splinters
pierced his skin, or when something
fell, and he, caught off guard,
had to stop it with his hands, the way I
felt I had to stop him in the hall,
keep him from my mother, bear
not just the force of his heavy arms,
but his excuse that he was only going
to the bathroom, and wanted nothing
to do with that *vieja*, because if he did
to her what his hands had done before,
I'd later take it as my job to comfort her,
to tend to what had swelled,
and remind her as much as I would
myself, that there was more than one way
for a body to be held.

Mercy

A man, she said. *Pegué un hombre.*
But when your mother stops,
steps out and ambles toward that dark
and bloodied mass, she finds instead
a dog, a stray that's wandered this far
from town, and that now, on a night
so humid, moonless, is your mother's
newest burden. And you remember Max,
the gashes on his neck and mouth,
the gnawed and broken ribs you touched,
fearing infections, rabies, or how,
if he survived, his body would be a ruin
of scars. And that night your mother
found you out back, asleep and clutching
what was once Max in your arms,
she knew one day she'd have to teach you
about loss, about that part of her life
when she, at the sun-seared edge
of her home country, had to leave things
behind—no stopping for whatever fell,
became a relic when it hit the ground.
There was no looking back,
and because she sees you seeing her,
she prays for this dying stray, hoping
that when she's done, both you and God
will accept why she's walked away.

Refuge

When they knock, we duck, hide
behind chairs, tables, the couch,
cram saliva and sentences back inside
our mouths. And when they knock again,
eager with rehearsed verses, pamphlets,
we tense our limbs, backs, stay silent
till their silhouettes scythe the curtains,
till the porch moans beneath their pious
steps, the way I imagine a porch,
at this moment, bearing the weight
of certain men: officers, agents,
uniformed shadows who search
the premises, hoping something here
yields a cache, or at least a man,
a woman, someone like my father
or mother, who, after crossing the border,
stumbled, fatigued and wet, toward
an abandoned house, praying, once inside,
that as the wind began to mimic voices,
their bodies wouldn't be tempted
to make a sound.

Fingernail

Not a head-turner, but long, sharp,
curved like a serpent's fang, and ready—
I thought—whenever he brought
his hand up, to strike a prey no one else
saw. And those days at his house,
with our mothers in the kitchen,
dishing secrets, gossip, I studied
Lalo's pinkie and nail, felt compelled
to imagine them as a wand, small
but useful enough to cast curses, spells,
or to help clear his desk, pour powder
from a bag, and with a quick scoop
"do a bump," which meant, from what
I knew, that he'd enter a different realm,
and that with every flick of the wrist,
nose rub and sniff, he was closer
to making himself disappear.

Herpes

As in a mouth sore. A blister
eating the edge of your lips.
As in a chance for your friends
to use their Cs from Sex Ed,
claim that you have it, that you
went down on one too many men.
And when their laughter settles,
and you resist the urge to say
something back, they guess,
from what they've read,
that you got it from your girl,
and she got it from her ex,
and he got it from the years
he slept around, shared his most
intimate fluids. Yes, it came
from him, and yes you ponder
the chances that after months
with your girlfriend, of backseat
make out sessions, of taking her lips
after kissing where you wanted her
to kiss, it would emerge now,
and like a parasite breaking free
from its host, blister your skin,
reminding you that you were never
immune, and that sometimes
pleasure is too good to be true.

Temptation

First he lets it dangle, swings it
by its tail. Then, when the snake rises,
hisses and slithers like fog between
the rocks, Lalo lifts the lid, lets
the mouse drop, and waits for
"nature to take its course."
And I think of Eve, temptation,
I think of cousins, like Lalo,
whose lives are about knives,
ninja stars, serpents. And I think,
as the hissing grows louder,
and the mouse scurries to the corner,
of my father at the river, watching
the wind scrawl its language
on the water, wondering,
if just beneath the oil-colored
surface, there's a snake waiting,
ready to strike. And though my father
never speaks of his crossing,
pretends there was no life before
and beyond that border, I picture him
dog-paddling to the edge, spitting
water from his mouth, and ignoring,
as best he could, a something
that grips his leg and promises,
with each squeeze and pull,
a reward his body shouldn't refuse.

Segue

Giddy, Mr. B entertains his tangent,
connects contraceptives to the animal
kingdom, then, without warning,
lectures on hyenas, explains their reproductive
systems, how the females have vaginas
that are fused, sealed, shut into more
synonyms than our bodies can feel.
And as he enlightens us on the pseudo penis,
lists facts with nods and hand movements,
you move into a tangent of your own,
return to a familiar trope, only this time
it's not your father you think about,
but your mother, young, cold, rushing
toward the river with her group, hoping
that the searchlights serrating the darkness
disappear, and that as she wades into
the water, offers the current her body,
she'll drift smoothly across, crawl onto
the bank, and, wrapped in an afterbirth
of moonlight, take her first steps
on this side of earth.

Leftovers

That which cannot be eaten lies
Last Supper-like among paper plates,
containers, yellow paper wrappers
speckled with mounds of ketchup,
chunks of warm lettuce, crumbs
of soggy bread. We open our plastic lids,
fork and scoop it in, stack it in the fridge,
and like every jar of jam, pickles, olives,
cherries, like the foil pans half-filled
with anonymous meat and chicken,
we forget it quickly, restack the Tupperware
it rests in, push it farther toward the back,
but never empty, never question why
it's still there—so long as something else
occupies the table, and hunger finds comfort
in another night of takeout, or those home-cooked
dinners I remember my mother feeding
my father every other evening, hoping
they'd offset a half-day of tying rebar,
sanding Sheetrock, pouring cement.
And though my parents sat in silence,
scraped everything off their plates,
I nibbled, saying I liked but was too full
to finish the leftover ground beef, potatoes,
canned corn and carrots, beans and weenies,
spaghetti and Hamburger Helper
we returned to at the end of the month,
microwaved that cold lump of mush,
milked a few meals out of one, and rationed
the only synonyms we knew for saving face,

the *good, sabroso, delicious* we uttered
to each other to show how stuffed our stomachs
were, and to persuade our mouths that with each
prolonged and labored chew, our food
was one bite closer to tasting good.

Coca-Cola

For dinner, birthday parties,
weddings where it took the place
of water, tea. For the afternoons
when you come in, sweaty from tackles,
home runs, from playing one-on-one
on the street, and fill your cup
from the 3 liter in the fridge,
that bottle you think of as the Holy Grail,
filled with a mixture that swallowed,
slushed against your teeth, leaves
you feeling resurrected, or at least
replenished, ready to go outside again,
face the heat, to wander from lot to lot,
unaware of the dangers of dehydration,
fatigue, or of why when you come back in,
pour your second cup, you meet
with your father's judgment, the stare
that says you'll never know what it means
to trek the edge of your home country,
and to have to piss on your shirt, convinced
that when you wring it, let the liquid
wash your lips, you'll forget
that you ever felt so thirsty.

Boils

They plagued the wrestlers first,
inflamed their necks, legs, arms.
Then, because we too tangled
our limbs—invented, when we slept
at each other's house, new games
for our flesh—the boils would strike us,
or so I thought, and told you, days
into the panic, that if we weren't already
infected, we would be soon enough.
So when the weekend came,
and the moment when one punch
would have led to a more complicated
touch, you insisted we stop, take off
our clothes, check the blind spots
on our backs, even if a mirror
could do the same job, though
we knew that once shirtless, bound
to the moment, it wouldn't matter that we
were boys, we weren't immune
to what impulses chose us to play out.

Psychic

And when prayers went unanswered,
and gossip no longer revealed
the epiphanies she desired, my mother
sat alone in the living room, flipped
through channel after channel, until Miss Cleo
appeared, and her phone number,
and my mother had to pick up the phone,
dial, explain her life, problems to Miss Cleo—
the fear that my father was cheating,
the *canas* she grew when I didn't listen,
the need to do something more than stay
at home all day, cooking, cleaning,
setting the table for dinner, even though
it was hours away, and even if all we did
was sit there, eat in silence, and then
go off to our separate corners, leaving TV
as the only option, and leaving me, the nights
I heard the commercials change from Spanish
to English, to watch her from the hall,
wonder why she was talking to the screen,
and if when she asked, *What do I do, Miss Cleo?*
¿Qué hago? the screen would answer back,
tell her, at last, her purpose.

VHS

The image blurs, and as gun fire
fades, and explosions warp,
a woman appears, in lingerie and heels,
ready for the man the scene cuts to,
for that body dying to be free
of clothes. Piece by piece they go,
and when all that's left is his birthday suit,
I know I'll never see the rest of *Die Hard*,
that my father, who bought the tape,
he claimed, to help him learn English,
was content with the English he knew,
and was willing to record over it,
not merely to succumb to temptation,
but to practice it, hide it from my mother,
convince us all he liked watching movies
late into the night, alone. And because
I wanted to see what he learned,
to know why, for months, his go-to line
was *Yippee ki-yay*, I took the film
from his closet, played it in the living room,
and sat awed not by McClane, but Hans
the villain, by that attitude that said
if you planned ahead, covered your tracks,
you could do what you wanted
and get away with it.

Seeds

Days, they said. *A week at most.*
And though you should have known,
should have seen past your cousins'
sarcasm, smirks, you thought about
how the seeds would grow, how they'd root
inside your gut, spread, sprout, until
a chain of baby watermelons had formed,
and with no place else to go, they'd stretch
and rip your insides apart. *Days*, they said.
A week, if you're lucky, is all you have.
And when they left, laughing and shaking
their heads, you ran behind your house,
stuffed your fingers inside your mouth,
and wondered, as the watermelon poured
past your lips as mush, what else had made
your stomach home: evening flies you sometimes
swallowed, spiders you thought stalked
your sleeping body at night, and which,
once past the tunnel of your throat,
filled your intestines with eggs—a fear
that left you feeling, as you threw up more,
that soon they'd hatch, and that once they did—
came out any way they could—you'd have
no choice but to become your mother,
to begin to worry, care, to do everything
to give them the life you never had.

Baywatch

But at the beach, in the deep end
by yourself, you suspect that if your legs
begin to cramp, and your arms lose
the will to move, there'll be no curvy
blonde lifeguard running toward you,
ready to risk her life for yours. No.
There'll be no crowd, screams,
no police sirens, yellow ribbons
to cordon off the scene. And as the waves
rise, push you farther out, the image
of wet breasts quickly fades,
and you remember how at the public pool,
young and convinced you lived
your past life as a fish, you suddenly
sank, watched the world darken, blur,
felt the back of your eyes sting, until,
near the bottom, a figure pulled you up,
placed you on the warm concrete,
and after checking your pulse, slapping
your cheeks, gave you mouth-to-mouth,
and with each long and worried breath,
made you believe their lips were those
of a woman, and made you pretend,
because a crowd was watching,
that when you opened your eyes,
saw the man's face, you were staring
at C.J. or Quinn, were being rewarded,
as you thought any boy would,
for knowledge your body
still lacked.

STROKE

You knew the verb,
how at home, alone,
you'd sit bathed
in the desktop's pink sunset,
stroke what you were too afraid
to name, just as your family
was too scared to say
the noun, as if your grandmother
would worsen, as if her face
would stay forever crooked,
like the portraits—as your cousins
claimed—of Picasso's mistresses,
only not as colorful, not known
by anyone but aunts, uncles
and grandchildren gathered
at the hospital, sitting in the lobby,
waiting to see everything
that happened, as though
her condition was a type
of show, a tragic piece of art
we could stare at, nod
in ways we told ourselves
we understood.

Pit Stop

All day you held it, squeezed
and prayed the feeling would pass,
that it wouldn't come to this:
silence, dusk, the side of some
deserted road, your pants down,
and you thinking—as you grip the roll,
tear sheets off—of your father
as lookout, of how you sense
he wants to laugh, yet how you know
that he too has done this, that before
you were born, he crossed into
this country, and throughout his trek,
when there was no town to rest,
no miracle of a bush or ditch,
he'd find a spot in the open, squat
and do his thing, never once thinking
that decades later, he'd watch his son,
after a day of hunting, take a shit,
that he'd have to yell to hurry up,
as though their lives depended on it.

Date Night

Besides the night you walked in,
saw your father on your mother,
saw as he—a heaving silhouette—
struggled to lift her leg, your parents
kept their distance, didn't touch,
didn't kiss, didn't speak to one another
if they could help it, instead asking
that you deliver their messages,
which you did, telling your mother
your father was hungry, telling your father
your mother had dinner ready.
And back and forth and back it went.
And as you grew with their silence,
you figured this too was a type of love,
that date nights were sitting on the couch,
watching *novelas*, gasping, laughing,
nodding off, and having the foresight
your mother had to drape your father—
when he was out cold—with a blanket,
knowing that when he awoke in the morning
for work, he'd owe her the same return.

La chupacabra

Another dead goat.
Another reason to believe
it was out there, skulking
in the fields, making—
with its jagged claws,
its sharp, mythic teeth—
a crime scene of its prey,
like what my father
found in the morning,
throat gnawed, belly torn
in half. And when I saw
the ribs—flesh hanging
from the ends—I thought
of the way my father ate,
how firmly he used his hands,
ripping through meat,
cramming charred and fatty
chunks inside his mouth,
just like *la chupacabra* would,
and just like I'd do until
my mother slapped my hand,
explained, with her stare alone,
that even if my father
snuck out late, came home
with blood on his shirt,
she'd be damned if I ate
like I've never been fed before.

Backtalk

One claimed they were hit
with a belt. Others a sandal,
extension chord, broom.
And because you wanted
to share their laughter,
their relief at escaping death
after every beating they took,
you invented your own,
how heavy your mother's hand
felt, how her callouses
were rough, like your father's,
only hers came—you imagined—
from hours of holding a frying
pan, cooking meal after meal
after meal. And your friends
believed you, never questioned,
never asked what happened
to the bruise, but you felt a slap
was too lenient, weak, and so,
to up the ante, you threw in
that frying pan, described
how your mother hurled it
at your head, and how,
because you had only a second
to duck, it scraped your scalp,
left a bump, made you proud
in ways your real mother
had yet to make you feel.

Ode to Glitter

Even after crayons, color pencils,
orange highlighter and the slow,
careful darkening of your best-ever
balloons, you knew it wouldn't do,
that that *Happy B-Day*—large, bold,
as black as your marker allowed—
wasn't enough. And so, before class
ended, you took the glitter without permission,
poured it on the letters full of glue,
and that afternoon at home, with your mother
in the kitchen, you presented her your card,
told yourself she loved it, even if she rushed
you out, complained of the glitter that fell
like rain on the floor. And oh how it decorated
the floors at school, how they were splayed
on Valentine's Day with red glitter,
pink glitter, glitter that stayed on your hands
for days, glitter you added on top of glitter
to show the girl you swore you'd spend
the rest of your life with how much you cared.
And what better way to prom-pose
than with glitter on a board, with your soul
mate's name written in gold, and feeling,
because it did the trick before, that once
you popped the question, revealed that shiny
lettering, you'd hear every answer but no.

Titanic

Though suspicious, my mother believed
I believed in history, that I was interested
in icebergs, ships, in the unsinkable
RMS Titanic, in the way the poor died
with the rich, in the passengers floating
all night, waiting for rescue boats,
or in how, as I stared at a frozen Jack
and Rose, I admired, even at my age,
the concept of love, and thought little
of Rose's breasts, or of how she laid
on her back, so free, so bare, so unlike
the pictures I tried to download at home,
and that, at the mercy of dial-up, froze
midway through, left me with my hand
in my shorts, and failed to keep me
as immersed as movies did, which is why
I begged to return, explaining that if I saw
these scenes again, I was bound to learn
something new.

Acknowledgments

Many thanks to the editors of the following magazines and journals in which some of these poems first appeared:

Booth: "Refuge"
Cold Mountain Review: "Piel"
Juke Joint: "AI," "Hair," "Hands" and "Mercy"
Lunch Ticket: "Golden Years"
The Rumpus: "MacGyver," "Ink," and "Onan"
Shenandoah: "Temptation"
Tar River Poetry: "Ode to Tupperware"
Twyckenham Notes: "K.O."

About the Author

Esteban Rodriguez is the author of *Dusk & Dust* and the microchapbook *Soledad*.

His poetry has appeared in *The Gettysburg Review, New England Review, Shenandoah, TriQuarterly,* The Rumpus, and elsewhere.

He is the Interviews Editor at the *EcoTheo Review* and is a regular reviews contributor at *PANK Magazine* and *Heavy Feather Review*.

He lives with his family and teaches high school in Austin, Texas.

www.ingramcontent.com/pod-product-compliance
Lightning Source LLC
Chambersburg PA
CBHW060506080526
44584CB00015B/1567